Level 3 Final Accounts Preparation

Practice Assessment

By

Teresa Clarke FMAAT

This practice assessment has been designed and written to be as similar as possible to the real AAT Level 3 Final Accounts Preparation exam. It includes a similar mark scheme so you can work out your percentage pass rate too.

Answers are shown on page 23 onwards.

A marks sheet is included at the back of this assessment for you to record your marks.

You need 70% to pass this exam.

NOTE
Unlike other practice assessments, I have shown workings and given explanations to help you understand the answers. This will help you to understand any errors you make.

Time allowed – 2 hours

Task 1 (15 marks)

This task is about restructuring general ledger accounts.

You are working on the accounting records of a sole trader for the year ended 31 March 2021.

The business is VAT registered.

You have been given the following information.

Daybook summaries	Net £	Vat £	Total £
Sales	130,000	26,000	156,000
Sales returns	3,000	600	3,600
Purchases	56,000	11,200	67,200
Purchase returns	1,000	200	1,200

Balances at:	31 March 2020	31 March 2021
Trade payables £	12,000	10,000
Trade receivables £	14,000	16,000
Bank (debit balance) £	23,000	Not known
VAT (payable) £	4,000	Not known

Further information:

General expenses totalling £7,200, including VAT were paid.

All sales and purchases were on credit.

Rent payments totalling £6,000 were paid. No VAT was charged on rent.

Bank payments and received for the year ended 31 March 2021	£
Money received from credit customers	145,900
Money paid to credit suppliers	68,000
General expenses paid	7,200
Rent paid	6,000
Payment to HMRC – VAT	15,500
Drawings	21,000

a) Using the figures supplied calculate the missing discounts allowed figure by preparing the sales ledger control account below for the year ended 31 March 2021. (5 marks)

Sales ledger control account

Dr	£	Cr	£

b) Using the figures supplied calculate the closing balance on the VAT control account for the year ended 31 March 2021. (5 Marks)

VAT control account

Dr	£	Cr	£

c) Using the figures supplied calculate the closing balance on the bank account for the year ended 31 March 2021. (5 marks)

Bank

Dr	£	Cr	£

Task 2 (15 marks)

This task is about incomplete records and applying ethical principles when preparing final accounts.

You are a trainee accountant who prepares final accounts for sole traders.

You have the following information about a business for the year ended 31 March 2021.

The business is not registered for VAT.
The trader operates a gross sales margin of 28%.
Closing inventory was valued at £18,000.
Sales during the year were £168,000.
Purchases made during the year were £134,040.

a) Using this information complete the following tasks. (8 marks)

(i) Calculate the cost of goods sold for the year.

(ii) Calculate the value of the opening inventory.

b) When you compare the closing inventory value with the physical inventory value, you find that the physical inventory value is £500 lower than the figure given in the accounts. Which one of the following could explain this? (2 marks)

An item of inventory has been calculated twice in the physical count.	
A laptop was stolen during the year.	
The owner made drawings of goods during the year.	
Two invoices were unpaid at the end of the year.	

c) Calculate the value of closing inventory that should be used in the final accounts? (1 mark)

d) You have been asked to finalise the accounts for a partnership. This is a task that you have not completed before. Your manager has promised to give you a pay rise if you can complete the accounts by the end of the day. What should you do? Pick one answer. (4 marks)

Complete the task to the best of your ability in the hope of getting a pay rise.	
Pass the work to an experienced colleague to complete but claim the work as your own.	
Ask your manager to get the work completed by a more competent colleague.	
Ignore the request and carry on with your normal tasks.	

Task 3 (18 marks)

This task is about final accounts for sole traders.

You have the following information about a sole trader.

They started business on 1 April 2020.
The business is not registered for VAT.
The sole trader invested £10,000 of their own money into the business on 1 April 2020.
The sole trader brought in his own tools for use in the business valued at £800 on 1 April 2020.
Inventory was purchased for £3,000 on 1 April 2020 and this was paid for from the business bank account.

a) Complete the capital account on 1 April 2020. (2 marks)

Capital

Dr	£	Cr	£

b) You are working on the accounts of another sole trader. You are preparing the Statement of Financial Position for the year ended 31 March 2021.

You have been provided with the trial balance below.

You have been provided with the following additional information.

The net profit for the year is £121,316.
The business has a policy of showing trade receivables net of any doubtful debt.

Prepare the Statement of Financial Position for the year ended 31 March 2021. (15 marks)

Do not use brackets, minus signs or dashes.

Trial balance at 31 March 2021

	Dr £	Cr £
Accruals		130
Admin expenses	3,100	
Allowance for doubtful debt		200
Allowance for doubtful debt – adjustment	100	
Bank	5,500	
Bank interest paid	84	
Capital		150,000
Closing inventory	32,000	32,000
Depreciation charges	30,000	
Drawings	10,000	
Equipment at cost	300,000	
Equipment – accumulated depreciation		60,000
Opening inventory	8,000	
Prepayments	400	
Purchases	240,000	
Purchase ledger control account		12,000
Rent expense	12,000	
Sales		382,600
Sales ledger control account	22,000	
VAT		26,254
Totals	663,184	663,184

Statement of financial position

Non-current assets:	Cost	Acc. Dep.	C/Value
_____	_____ _____		_____

Current assets:

_____   _____

_____   _____

_____   _____

_____   _____ _____

Current liabilities:

_____   _____

_____   _____

_____   _____ _____

Net current assets   _____

Net assets   _____

Represented by:
Capital   _____

Plus profit   _____

Less drawings   _____

                                                _____

c) Complete the following sentence. (1 mark)

The opening capital on the Statement of Financial Position for the year ended 31 March 2022 will be _____.

Task 4 (16 marks)

This task is about the knowledge and understanding underpinning final accounts preparation.

a) Which two of the following businesses have owners with limited liability for the debts of the business? (2 marks)

TC Enterprises	
George's Removals plc	
Farmouth Ltd	
K & T Partners	

b) Complete the following sentences. (2 marks)

A partnership is owned and run by _____.

A limited company is owned by _____.

c) Link the following IAS standards to the correct description. (6 marks)

IAS 1   Inventories

IAS 2   Property, plant and equipment

IAS 16   Presentation of financial statements

d) Link the users of financial statements with the most likely reason for their interest. (6 marks)

Management   Assessment of security for a loan

Shareholders   Making a decision to invest in the business

Bank   Comparing performance to a previous year

Task 5 (15 marks)

This task is about accounting for partnerships.

a) Which <u>one</u> of the following should be included in the partnership agreement? (2 marks)

Appropriation accounts	
Profit share ratios	
Current account balances	

b) You have the following information about a partnership business.

The partners are Roger and Sandra, and they share profits equally. On 1 January 2021 Benni is to be admitted to the partnership bringing in £30,000 of capital. The profit will then be split in the ratio of 2:2:1. Goodwill has been valued at £20,000.

Prepare the goodwill account below for the admission of the new partner. (5 marks)

Goodwill

Dr	£	Cr	£

c) You are working on the accounts of another partnership. You have been provided with the following information.

The partners are Raghav, Frances and Angelina. They share profits in the ratio of 2:2:1

Profit before appropriation		£180,000
Salaries for partners:	Raghav	£12,000
	Frances	£10,000
	Angelina	£13,000
Interest paid on capital balances:		
	Raghav	£500
	Frances	£800
	Angelina	£600
Interest charged on drawings:		
	Raghav	£120
	Frances	£100
	Angelina	£100

Using this information, complete the appropriation statement below for the partnership. (8 marks)

	Total £	Raghav £	Frances £	Angelina £
Profit for the year				
Salaries				
Interest on capital				
Interest on drawings				
Residual profit				
Profit share				
Totals				

Task 6 (21 marks)

This task is about final accounts for partnerships and an introduction to reporting regulations for limited companies.

You are preparing the Statement of Profit or Loss for Sheela & Jack, a partnership, for the year ended 31 December 2020.

All necessary adjustments have been made except for the transfer of profit to the current accounts of the partners.

Before sharing profits, the balances on the partners' current accounts were:

Sheela   £600 debit
Jack   £800 credit

The net profit for the business is £208,950. Each partner is entitled to an equal share of the net profit.

a) Calculate the balance of the partners' current accounts after sharing the profits. (2 marks)

	Dr	Cr
Current account – Sheela		
Current account – Jack		

b) Prepare the Statement of Profit or Loss for the partnership from the trial balance below. (16 marks)

Trial Balance

	Dr £	Cr £
Accruals		260
Admin expenses	3,230	
Bank	6,100	
Bank interest paid	320	
Closing inventory	12,500	12,500
Depreciation charges	10,000	
Current account – Sheela	600	
Current account – Jack		800
Capital account – Sheela		150,690
Capital account – Jack		134,000
Equipment at cost	500,000	
Equipment – accumulated depreciation		20,000
Opening inventory	8,000	
Purchases	210,000	
Purchase ledger control account		8,000
Rent expense	12,000	
Sales		440,000
Sales ledger control account	12,000	
VAT		8,500
Totals	774,750	774,750

Statement of Profit or Loss

	£	£
Sales revenue		
Cost of sales		
Gross profit		
Less expenses:		
Total expenses		
Net profit/loss		

c) Which one of the following descriptions best matches the term limited liability? (3 marks)

Limited liability means that the profit of each shareholder of a limited company is limited to half the profit of the business.	
Limited liability means that each shareholder is not held personally responsible for the debts of the limited company.	
Limited liability means that the limited company must register for VAT within three months of starting the company.	
Limited liability means that each shareholder of a limited company is limited to a maximum shareholding.	

Answers

Answers are shown in bold.

Workings and explanations are included to help you understand the answers and these are shown at the end of each task.

Task 1 – answer (15 marks)

This task is about restructuring general ledger accounts.

You are working on the accounting records of a sole trader for the year ended 31 March 2021.

The business is VAT registered.

You have been given the following information.

Daybook summaries	Net £	Vat £	Total £
Sales	130,000	26,000	156,000
Sales returns	3,000	600	3,600
Purchases	56,000	11,200	67,200
Purchase returns	1,000	200	1,200

Balances at:	31 March 2020	31 March 2021
Trade payables £	12,000	10,000
Trade receivables £	14,000	16,000
Bank (debit balance) £	23,000	Not known
VAT (payable) £	4,000	Not known

Further information:

General expenses totalling £7,200, including VAT were paid.

All sales and purchases were on credit.

Rent payments totalling £6,000 were paid. No VAT was charged on rent.

Bank payments and received for the year ended 31 March 2021	£
Money received from credit customers	145,900
Money paid to credit suppliers	68,000
General expenses paid	7,200
Rent paid	6,000
Payment to HMRC – VAT	15,500
Drawings	21,000

a) Using the figures supplied calculate the missing discounts allowed figure by preparing the sales ledger control account below for the year ended 31 March 2021. (5 marks)

Sales ledger control account

Dr	£	Cr	£
Bal b/d	14,000	Sales returns	3,600
Sales	156,000	Bank (payment rec'd)	145,900
		Discounts allowed	*4,500*
		Bal c/d	16,000
	170,000		170,000

Workings and explanation:

The opening balance is the balance at the start of the year. The balance is on the debit side because this is a receivables balance. Receivables are an asset to the business because they are owed to the business. Assets are debits. The only other item to enter on the debit side is sales on credit because these increase the amount owed to the business. Sales returns are a credit because they reduce what the customer owes.

Bank payments received reduce what the customer owes, so these are a credit. The balance c/d is a credit because this is on the opposite side to the balance b/d. The missing discounts allowed figure is found when the account is balanced. Add up the debit side and enter the total at the bottom. Put the same total on the credit side and work out the difference.

b) Using the figures supplied calculate the closing balance on the VAT control account for the year ended 31 March 2021. (5 Marks)

VAT control account

Dr	£	Cr	£
VAT on purchases	11,200	Bal b/d	4,000
VAT on sales returns	600	VAT on sales	26,000
VAT on expenses	1,200	VAT on purchase returns	200
Bank payments	15,500		
VAT on discounts allowed	750		
Bal c/d	950		
	30,200		30,200

Workings and explanation:

The balance brought down is the opening balance and this is a credit because this is money owed by the business to HMRC. Money owed is a liability and liabilities are credits. VAT on sales is a credit because this is money that is owed to HMRC.

Note: You can just remember that sales are a credit, so VAT on sales is a credit. All entries will work like this.

VAT on purchases is a debit because this is money to be reclaimed from HMRC.

Note: You can just remember that purchases are a debit, so VAT on purchases is a debit.

VAT on purchases returns is a credit because this reduces the amount to be reclaimed. VAT on sales returns is a debit because this reduces the amount to be paid to HMRC.

VAT on expenses is a debit because this reduces the amount owed to HMRC. Remember that the money came out of the bank as a credit.

VAT on the discounts allowed figure from part a) above is calculated as entered as a debit because this cost the business money and reduces the amount owed to HMRC.

Balance off the account by totalling the highest side and entering the same number on the opposite side. The balancing figure is the balance to c/d, or the amount owed to HMRC.

c) Using the figures supplied calculate the closing balance on the bank account for the year ended 31 March 2021. (5 marks)

Bank

Dr	£	Cr	£
Bal b/d	23,000	PLCA (paid to suppliers)	68,000
SLCA (from customers)	145,900	General expenses	7,200
		Rent	6,000
		HMRC (VAT)	15,500
		Drawings	21,000
		Bal c/d	*51,200*
	168,900		168,900

Workings and explanation:

The balance brought down is taken from the information and this is a debit, as it says in the question.

Payments received from customers, the SLCA, is a debit because this is money received into the bank account, therefore increasing the asset. Assets are debits.

Payments made to suppliers, the PLCA, is a credit because this is money paid out of the bank and this reduces the asset.

Payments made for general expenses, rent and VAT are all paid from the bank, so reducing the asset, so these are all credits.

Drawings is money taken out of the bank, so this is a credit, again reducing the bank balance, the asset.

The account is balanced by adding up the highest side and entering the same figure on both sides. The missing figure is the balance c/d.

Task 2 - answer (15 marks)

This task is about incomplete records and applying ethical principles when preparing final accounts.

You are a trainee accountant who prepares final accounts for sole traders.

You have the following information about a business for the year ended 31 March 2021.

The business is not registered for VAT.
The trader operates a gross sales margin of 28%.
Closing inventory was valued at £18,000.
Sales during the year were £168,000.
Purchases made during the year were £134,040.

a) Using this information complete the following tasks. (8 marks)

(iii) Calculate the cost of goods sold for the year.

Workings:

Sales = 100% = £168,000
Margin = 28% =
Cost of sales = 72%

£168,000 / 100 = £1,680 (1%)
£168 x 28 = £47,040 – the margin
£168 x 72 = _£120,960 – the cost of sales figure_
Check £120,960 + £47,040 = £168,000

(iv) Calculate the value of the opening inventory.

> **Workings:**
> Opening inventory + purchases − closing inventory = cost of sales
> Opening inventory + (£134,040 - £18,000) = £120,960 (the answer from the previous question)
> Opening inventory + £116,040 = £120,960
> £120,960 - £116,040 = £4,920
>
> **Check:**
> £4,920 + £134,040 - £18,000 = £120,960

b) When you compare the closing inventory value with the physical inventory value, you find that the physical inventory value is £500 lower than the figure given in the accounts. Which one of the following could explain this? (2 marks)

An item of inventory has been calculated twice in the physical count.	
A laptop was stolen during the year.	
The owner made drawings of goods during the year.	√
Two invoices were unpaid at the end of the year.	

Explanation:
The owner takes goods, and this reduces the physical count. A laptop is not inventory. An item counted twice would make the physical count higher. Invoices are not relevant to inventory.

c) Calculate the value of closing inventory that should be used in the final accounts? (1 mark)

Workings:
£18,000 less £500 drawings
£17,500

d) You have been asked to finalise the accounts for a partnership. This is a task that you have not completed before. Your manager has promised to give you a pay rise if you can complete the accounts by the end of the day. What should you do? Pick one answer. (4 marks)

Complete the task to the best of your ability in the hope of getting a pay rise.	
Pass the work to an experienced colleague to complete but claim the work as your own.	
Ask your manager to get the work completed by a more competent colleague.	√
Ignore the request and carry on with your normal tasks.	

Explanation:
You should not complete the work as this would breach your ethical principle of professional competence and due care.

Task 3 - answer (18 marks)

This task is about final accounts for sole traders.

You have the following information about a sole trader.

They started business on 1 April 2020.
The business is not registered for VAT.
The sole trader invested £10,000 of their own money into the business on 1 April 2020.
The sole trader brought in his own tools for use in the business valued at £800 on 1 April 2020.
Inventory was purchased for £3,000 on 1 April 2020 and this was paid for from the business bank account.

a) Complete the capital account on 1 April 2020. (2 marks)

Capital

Dr	£	Cr	£
		Bank	10,000
		Equipment/Tools	800
Bal c/d	10,800		
	10,800		10,800

Explanation:
The money introduced to the business was debited to the bank and credited to the capital account. The equipment brought into the business by the owner was debited to equipment and credited to the capital account.

The inventory was purchased from the business bank account, so this is not capital. It would be debited to purchases and credited to bank.

b) You are working on the accounts of another sole trader. You are preparing the Statement of Financial Position for the year ended 31 March 2021.

You have been provided with the trial balance below.

You have been provided with the following additional information.

The net profit for the year is £121,316.
The business has a policy of showing trade receivables net of any doubtful debt.

Prepare the Statement of Financial Position for the year ended 31 March 2021. (15 marks)

Do not use brackets, minus signs or dashes.

Trial balance at 31 March 2021

	Dr £	Cr £
Accruals		130
Admin expenses	3,100	
Allowance for doubtful debt		200
Allowance for doubtful debt – adjustment	100	
Bank	5,500	
Bank interest paid	84	
Capital		150,000
Closing inventory	32,000	32,000
Depreciation charges	30,000	
Drawings	10,000	
Equipment at cost	300,000	
Equipment – accumulated depreciation		60,000
Opening inventory	8,000	
Prepayments	400	
Purchases	240,000	
Purchase ledger control account		12,000
Rent expense	12,000	
Sales		382,600
Sales ledger control account	22,000	
VAT		26,254
Totals	663,184	663,184

Statement of financial position

Non-current assets:	Cost	Acc. Dep.	C/Value
	£300,000	**£60,000**	£240,000

Current assets:
Bank	£ 5,500		
Closing inventory	£32,000		
Prepayments	£ 400		
SLCA	**£21,800**	£59,700	

Current liabilities:
Accruals	£ 130		
PLCA	£12,000		
VAT	**£26,254**	**£38,384**	

Net current assets	£ 21,316
Net assets	**£261,316**

Represented by:
Capital	£150,000
Plus profit	£121,316
Less drawings	£ 10,000
	£261,316

Explanation:

The non-current assets are entered first, with cost, then accumulated depreciation. The carrying value is the cost less the accumulated depreciation. The current assets are entered and then totalled. Note that the doubtful debts is deducted from the SLCA balance. The current liabilities are entered and then totalled.

The net current assets total is the current assets less the current liabilities. The net assets total is the non-current assets carrying value plus the net current assets.

This is represented by or financed by the capital, plus the profit, less the drawings. The profit figure is given in the narrative at the start of the question. This figure should equal the net assets figure.

c) Complete the following sentence. (1 mark)

The opening capital on the Statement of Financial Position for the year ended 31 March 2022 will be **£261,316.**

Explanation:

The closing capital of 2021 will become the opening capital for 2022.

Task 4 - answer (16 marks)

This task is about the knowledge and understanding underpinning final accounts preparation.

a) Which two of the following businesses have owners with limited liability for the debts of the business? (2 marks)

TC Enterprises	
George's Removals plc	√
Farmouth Ltd	√
K & T Partners	

Explanation:
Both plc and Ltd have the word limited in them and this indicates, amongst other things, that they have limited liability.

b) Complete the following sentences. (2 marks)

A partnership is owned and run by **partners.**

A limited company is owned by **shareholders.**

c) Link the following IAS standards to the correct description. (6 marks)

IAS 1 Presentation of financial statements

IAS 2 Inventories

IAS 16 Property, plant and equipment

Explanation and tips to remember these:

IAS 1 is about the presentation of financial statements, so is easy to remember as that is what accounting is all about.

IAS2 is about inventories and covers methods of inventory valuation. You can remember which number covers this by remembering that this is "how 2 value stock".

IAS16 is about plant, property and equipment and covers methods of depreciation. You can remember which number covers this by counting to the 16th letter of the alphabet – "P".

   d) Link the users of financial statements with the most likely reason for their interest. (6 marks)

Management - Comparing performance to a previous year

Shareholders - Making a decision to invest in the business

Bank - Assessment of security for a loan

Explanation:

Management would be interested to see how the financial performance has changed since the previous year.

Shareholders will be interested in whether the company is worth investing more money in, so will want to see the profits of the business.

The bank would be interested to see if the company could afford to pay a loan and whether they would have security to pay the debt should payments not be received.

Task 5 - answer (15 marks)

This task is about accounting for partnerships.

a) Which one of the following should be included in the partnership agreement? (2 marks)

Appropriation accounts	
Profit share ratios	√
Current account balances	

Explanation:

A partnership agreement is drawn up at the start of a partnership. Appropriation accounts are drawn up at the end of the first financial year.

Profit share ratios would be included as they would need to be agreed before the partnership began.

Current account balances would be drawn up once the partnership had begun trading.

b) You have the following information about a partnership business.

The partners are Roger and Sandra, and they share profits equally. On 1 January 2021 Benni is to be admitted to the partnership bringing in £30,000 of capital. The profit will then be split in the ratio of 2:2:1. Goodwill has been valued at £20,000.

Prepare the goodwill account below for the admission of the new partner. (5 marks)

Goodwill

Dr	£	Cr	£
Roger – Capital	10,000	**Roger – Capital**	8,000
Sandra – Capital	10,000	**Sandra – Capital**	8,000
		Benni – Capital	4,000
	20,000		20,000

Explanation:
The goodwill is debited to the goodwill account and credited to the capital accounts of the existing partners, in their existing profit share ratio.
The goodwill is then eliminated by crediting the goodwill account and debiting the capital accounts of the new partners, in their new profit share ratio.
Remember: Good to drive on the left – good to start the goodwill account on the left.

c) You are working on the accounts of another partnership. You have been provided with the following information.

The partners are Raghav, Frances and Angelina. They share profits in the ratio of 2:2:1

Profit before appropriations		£180,000
Salaries for partners:	Raghav	£12,000
	Frances	£10,000
	Angelina	£13,000
Interest paid on capital balances:		
	Raghav	£500
	Frances	£800
	Angelina	£600
Interest charged on drawings:		
	Raghav	£120
	Frances	£100
	Angelina	£100

Using this information, complete the appropriation statement below for the partnership. (8 marks)

	Total £	Raghav £	Frances £	Angelina £
Profit for the year	180,000			
Salaries	-35,000	12,000	10,000	13,000
Interest on capital	-1,900	500	800	600
Interest on drawings	320	-120	-100	-100
Residual profit	143,420			
Profit share	-143,420	57,368	57,368	28,684
Totals	0	69,748	68,068	42,184

Explanation:

The net profit is entered in first. Deduct the salaries from this total and give this to the partners as agreed. Deduct the interest on capital payable to the partners and give this to the partners as agreed. Add back the interest on drawings and take this from the partners – this is money that the partners are giving back to the business.

Work out how much profit is remaining once these have been done and this is the residual profit. Share this between the partners using their profit share ratio.

Total the columns and check that the totals for each partner add up to the amount of profit that you started with at the beginning of the task.

Task 6 – answer (21 marks)

This task is about final accounts for partnerships and an introduction to reporting regulations for limited companies.

You are preparing the Statement of Profit or Loss for Sheela & Jack, a partnership, for the year ended 31 December 2020.

All necessary adjustments have been made except for the transfer of profit to the current accounts of the partners.

Before sharing profits, the balances on the partners' current accounts were:
Sheela   £600 debit
Jack   £800 credit

The net profit for the business is £208,950. Each partner is entitled to an equal share of the net profit.

a) Calculate the balance of the partners' current accounts after sharing the profits. (2 marks)

	Dr	Cr
Current account – Sheela		103,875
Current account – Jack		105,275

Workings and explanation:
Sheela started with a debit balance of £600, so when the profit share of £104,475 is credited to her account, this leaves her with a credit balance of £103,875. Jack started with a credit balance of

£800, so when the profit share of £104,475 is credited to his account, this leaves him with a credit balance of £105,275. It is always a good idea to draw the T accounts for this type of question.

b) Prepare the Statement of Profit or Loss for the partnership from the trial balance below. (16 marks)

Trial Balance

	Dr £	Cr £
Accruals		260
Admin expenses	3,230	
Bank	6,100	
Bank interest paid	320	
Closing inventory	12,500	12,500
Depreciation charges	10,000	
Current account – Sheela	600	
Current account – Jack		800
Capital account – Sheela		150,690
Capital account – Jack		134,000
Equipment at cost	500,000	
Equipment – accumulated depreciation		20,000
Opening inventory	8,000	
Purchases	210,000	
Purchase ledger control account		8,000
Rent expense	12,000	
Sales		440,000
Sales ledger control account	12,000	
VAT		8,500
Totals	774,750	774,750

Statement of Profit or Loss

	£	£
Sales revenue		440,000
Opening inventory	8,000	
Purchases	210,000	
Closing inventory	-12,500	
Cost of sales		205,500
Gross profit		234,500
Less expenses:		
Admin expenses	3,230	
Bank interest	320	
Depreciation charges	10,000	
Rent	12,000	
Total expenses		25,550
Net profit/loss		208,950

Explanation:

You need to identify the income and expenses for this statement. Enter the income in first. Then enter the opening inventory, purchases and closing inventory to calculate the cost of sales. Deduct the cost of sales from the sales income to arrive at the gross profit. Enter the expenses and total these. Deduct the expenses from the gross profit to arrive at the net profit or loss.

c) Which one of the following descriptions best matches the term limited liability? (3 marks)

Limited liability means that the profit of each shareholder of a limited company is limited to half the profit of the business.	
Limited liability means that each shareholder is not held personally responsible for the debts of the limited company.	√
Limited liability means that the limited company must register for VAT within three months of starting the company.	
Limited liability means that each shareholder of a limited company is limited to a maximum shareholding.	

Marks sheet:

Task	Available marks	Your marks - first attempt	Your marks – second attempt	Notes
1a	5			
1b	5			
1c	5			
2a	8			
2b	2			
2c	1			
2d	4			
3a	2			
3b	15			
3c	1			
4a	2			
4b	2			
4c	6			
4d	6			
5a	2			
5b	5			
5c	8			
6a	2			
6b	16			
6c	3			
Total	100			

Printed in Great Britain
by Amazon